Book Dedication

To my darling JAS who has brought so much clarity and purpose to my life.

For my first born Zerlinda, I am so proud of the young lady she is becoming.

AND

Darlene whose sincere affirmation at Nappywood 2015 finally gave me the urgency I required to finally concretize my thoughts on these digital, and sometime paper, pages.

SEO Training 2017 Introduction

Thank you for purchasing this book, SEO Training 2017: Search Engine Optimization and Marketing for Small Business. I wrote this book to help students, business owners, marketing managers, and marketing executives understand why and how digital marketing and search engine optimization is important and can support sales activity and drive revenue.

Hello, my name is Zhe L. Scott, MPP[1]. I am a Marketing Strategist, Digital & SEO Marketing Expert, Digital Marketing Professor for Simplilearn.com, Serial Entrepreneur, and Professional Violinist. After graduating from Long Beach Polytechnic High School, I left home to study on the east coast. I worked hard and earned a Bachelor's of Science in Management Science with an emphasis in Information Technology, and a Bachelor's of Science in Music from the Massachusetts Institute of Technology.

While I was at MIT I built my first website using HTML in the fall of 1996. Later I took classes at the Sloan School of Management in website building, innovation, and various information technology topics.

---

[1] MPP stands for Masters of Arts in Public Policy.

After my studies at the Massachusetts Institute of Technology in Cambridge, Massachusetts I worked for a Fortune 500 Company named Raytheon for one year, and in nine months I was identified as a high potential, but I wanted more. I wanted more than the certain success of corporate life at Raytheon building web applications in Command, Communication, and Control in Waltham, Massachusetts.

I yearned to contribute and help in a more direct way, in the lives of people professionally. Just like a musician directly touches the lives of those that they perform in front of. So, after I finished one year of work at Raytheon, I decided to attend the Ford School of Public Policy at University of Michigan. I am proud to have earned my Master of Arts in Public Policy from the Ford School.

The experience of living and working in the East Coast, West Coast, and Midwest has given me a unique perspective on the American business landscape. When it comes to my professional life, I firmly believe that small business owners need as much support as possible. **The purpose of this book is to help you improve your marketing.** *My intent is to help as many small businesses as possible increase their visibility to the maximum number of ideal prospects for their product or service.* I want businesses to make more sales so that they see an increase in their revenue stream. I want small businesses to have more leads, and more revenue. When small businesses thrive, the people get jobs, and communities prosper. I have seen it time and time again. That is my intent and catalyst for writing this book. I want you to apply the techniques within these pages to grow your business.

I know what it feels like to not be seen, heard, or valued. When I was working as a SEO and Sales Manager at a Digital Marketing company in 2010-2012 I built the company from $0 in recurring revenue to $500,000/year in recurring revenue. However, I had a secret, that I was deeply ashamed and frustrated with. I was on food stamps. I was an MIT graduate, talking to business owners all over the world, but I had to fill out food stamp applications to be able to eat every month so I could pay all of my bills. Now, I know what you might be thinking. You are thinking that my negotiation skills must really suck. Well when I started working for another digital marketing agency in California in 2015 I communicated clearly to the hiring manager at the time that I would not work for them for less than $60,000/year. Three months later my compensation changed, and I was shocked. It went from $60,000/year to $40,000/year plus 5% commission on my entire book of business that I serviced. I later found out that the link building department was turned off and so all of my efforts to stabilize my income under the changed compensation structure was not fully supported by management. THIS is why I had to start my company. TSQ Marketing Inc was incorporated in January 2017. I KNOW what it feels like to not be seen, heard and valued, and that is why I am providing the knowledge and experience in this book to empower your marketing so that you can bring your vision to market in a big way.

When I was building the recurring revenue at a previous digital marketing agency from $0 to $500K I started a blog called Lady Zhe on Seo Services. I started that blog to draw attention to my employer at that time. After deciding to step out on faith and take 100% responsibility and control of my own professional endeavors I referred to that blog as a starting point for this book. This book highlights my knowledge and experience obtained as I successfully executed digital marketing campaigns in my career. From 2010 to the present I have helped over 200 business get to the top of their niche, and on to Google Page 1. I have managed multiple digital marketing campaigns in a plethora of verticals including and not limited to: clothing and accessories, auto, fashion, tourism, manufacturing, and professional services. This book is a compilation of my experience built on the foundation of my blog writing from many years ago.

Why this trip down memory lane? I want you to have context for this book. I want you to believe and understand that I can help you. I have been active on the internet since 1996. I have seen it truly evolve tremendously over time and I know how you feel as a business owner when you are not being seen, heard and valued in the market place. I want to help.

Who Is this Book Ideal for?

The purpose of this book is to help small businesses. Small business owners, entrepreneurs, and employees with limited marketing budgets, but remain committed to growing their marketing capabilities are the target audience for this book. Small business owners short on money, but are willing to spend the time to develop a viable digital marketing strategy are whom this book has been written for. The steps outlined in this book are feasible and are not overwhelming or impossible to implement.

I realize that everyone is not ready for the internet of things. Besides, many business owners and employees have their hands full and do not want to add anything frivolous to their plates. However, we live in a world with smart watches, home appliances, smart TVs, smart cars, and more. Everything has to be connected to data and information in the cloud (i.e. GPS). I know technophobes do exist, however it's time to understand how the internet can and should be leveraged for your brand to increase your revenue streams.

This book is for the small business owners[2] who need to improve the efficacy of their digital strategy on the World Wide Web (WWW) to drive their company revenue themselves. There is absolutely no point in engaging in a flurry of activity that yields no fruit or monetary gain. Spending time and money with no return on investment must be avoided by small business owners at all costs.

Whether you are a business owner who needs more customers, sales, or leads; this book is for you. If you are new to SEO, thinking about a career in digital marketing, then this book is also for you. A short while after TV killed the radio star, the internet has made advertising on TV obsolete. Consumers, customers, and businesses that are looking for products and services now turn to the search engines on their computers, smart phones and social media accounts to procure the information that they require.

---

[2] Small Business Owner: Solopreneur or business that has revenues south of one million dollars a year.

In an October 22, 2013 article in Forbes Magazine[3] the headline blared, "Brands Moving Budgets from TV to Online Video". Reading the article gives tangible proof to the trend that consumers are not watching television as much, but are on the internet, social media, and smart phone applications. In addition, I have spoken to hundreds of business owners and employees worldwide. Many business owners from construction contracting, pest control, software development, investment, real estate, Attorneys, Jewelry, Clothing, and various business consultants find that they are spending more on trade shows; less on the yellow pages or phone book. They are spending much more of their time and effort on developing a professional website, social media marketing, search engine optimization, and using alternative digital marketing techniques such as email marketing as well.

---

[3] http://www.forbes.com/sites/roberthof/2013/10/22/brands-moving-budgets-from-tv-to-online-video/

I have managed one or more campaigns in the following verticals:

Arts and Entertainment	Internet and Telecom
Automotive	Jobs and Education
Beauty and Fitness	Law and Government
Books and Literature	Online Communities
Business and Industrial Markets	People and Society
Computers and Electronics	Pets and Animals
Finance	Real Estate
Food and Beverage	Reference
Games	Science
Healthcare	Shopping
Hobbies and Leisure	Sports
Home and Garden	Travel
	Other

This book has over 99 ways to improve your digital marketing's effectiveness. Whether you are seeking to expand your reach from a brick and mortar to the virtual world or a small business with a website that needs to be improved, this book is for you. I cover the basics of the working of the internet, open source tools and instructions on how to install them on your computer, and marketing strategies that work. This book is a manual that will walk you through the successful implementation of effective digital marketing strategies. I want your digital marketing to go smooth.

A technical side note: I use a PC for the majority of the advanced tools that I use for my clients. However, here is a list of platform independent tools (i.e. a Mac user or a PC user can use them) that I sincerely recommend that you obtain and install on your computer. Installing these software packages will allow you to fully implement the recommendations of this SEO Training Guide. I will explain how to execute strategies here via these basic tools.

Platform Independent Productivity Tools that Work!

Only Office
(https://onlyoffice.org)
According to its website, ONLYOFFICE™ is a feature-rich office suite that enables you to store and co-edit documents, manage projects, email correspondence and customer relations in one place.

Carter Cole's SEO Site Tools Chrome Plugin
(http://blog.cartercole.com/2010/02/seo-site-tools-chrome-seo-extension.html)
Is a great way to look at a web page's meta data, number of pages indexing, backlinks, and more. With just a click you can get simple, yet valuable insight into the health and SEO power of

a website when you are using the Google Chrome Web Browser. This tool also gives you data on the impact of your social media marketing efforts.

Google Keyword Tool
(https://adwords.google.com/ko/KeywordPlanner/Home
Google says: *that their Keyword Planner is like a workshop for building new Search Network campaigns or expanding existing ones. You can search for keyword and ad group ideas, get historical statistics, see how a list of keywords might perform and even create a new keyword list by multiplying several lists of keywords together. A free AdWords tool, Keyword Planner can also help you choose competitive bids and budgets to use with your campaigns.*

Please note that if you do not have a Google AdWords you will have to start an account to take advantage of the free data available in this tool. That just means that you have to create an ad campaign and add a payment method. Please note that if you do not add a payment method or turn on a campaign, you will only get the search volumes by range. (i.e. 10-100, 1K-10K, etc.). You will also need a Gmail address for the easiest access of this and all of Google's free platforms. You can go to www.gmail.com to create your free email address.

This eBook does not teach you how to use the internet, a computer, or code. This eBook does not instruct you how to

set up your social media accounts. However, this book will give insight into tried and true digital marketing strategies I use to get additional visibility for over 200 website marketing campaigns worldwide.

What you will achieve after you read and internalize the knowledge in this book will help you to assess the competitiveness of your niche and develop and implement strategies to get improved keyword placement and traffic for your company website. This book will also help you identify key issues, challenges, and technical concerns that are preventing you from obtaining the level of demand generation that you need to hit your revenue goals.

Discover where you are on your digital marketing journey, and use the principles in this SEO Training Guide to develop effective tactics to apply in your digital marketing activities. Just reading and reflecting on this content will have little effect on your marketing until you convert these "thoughts' into action by re-visiting your goals, amending and implementing your marketing action plan every week for the year ahead.

As this book continues you will see the following symbol:

 The Takeaway Activity. When you see this symbol throughout the book. Pause & Reflect. Make notes, Answer the Question or Complete the exercise. This will greatly assist you.

If you need additional help, guidance or support then my contact details are at the end of the book, and please accept my invitation to join my online community of others who have read my book and who share, practice and benefit from the applied principles of SEO Training 2017.

Ready? Now, let's make the next 12 months, the best you've ever had...

Zhe L. Scott
www.theseoqueen.net
September, 2017

ISBN: 9781549766619

Copyright Notice

© Zhe L. Scott, 2015 - 2017

All rights reserved. No part of this book may be reproduced in any form or by any electronic or mechanical means including information storage and retrieval systems – except in the case of brief quotations in articles or reviews – without the permission in writing from its publisher.

Table of Contents

Book Dedication

SEO Training 2017 Introduction

Who Is this Book Ideal for?

Platform Independent Productivity Tools that Work!

Copyright Notice

Table of Contents

The Internet and Modern Marketing Methods

Keyword Research: How Your Ideal Prospects Find You

On-Page Implementation Success

Off Page Implementation Success

Social Media: The Essential Social Profiles

Traffic and Troubleshooting

Tracking and Analytics Tools

One Last Thing...

About the Author

Other Work by the Author

Credits

Need More Website Traffic?

The Internet and Modern Marketing Methods

The Internet

The Internet has leveled the business playing field. If you understand how the internet works you can put your products and services in front of hundreds, thousands, or millions of prospects that want your exact product or service at that exact moment they are ready to buy.

Since the Industrial Age, physical resources and capital ownership were the ONLY way to market to the masses. The high cost of printing, radio, and television made it tough for entry and stability in the marketplace. Now, with the internet you can target everyone. You can even customize the buying experience.

All the various types of digital marketing are important, but would be absolutely impossible without the advent of the search engine. I remember when Dogpile and AltaVista were the rage. Those were the days. I also remember when Yahoo was the directory or search tool that I used to look up any and everything. Now the search landscape has changed.

What is a Search Engine?

A Search Engine organizes websites and gives the user the most relevant website content for a given query. According to eBizMBA.com[4] the 10 Most Popular Search Engines are as follows:

1. Google: 1,600,000,000 Estimated Unique Monthly Visitors
2. Bing: 400,000,000 Estimated Unique Monthly Visitors
3. Yahoo: 300,000,000 Estimated Unique Monthly Visitors
4. Ask: 245,000,000 Estimated Unique Monthly Visitors
5. AOL Search: 124,000,000 Estimated Unique Monthly Visitors
6. Wow: 100,000,000 Estimated Unique Monthly Visitors
7. WebCrawler: 65,000,000 Estimated Unique Monthly Visitors
8. MyWebSearch: 60,000,000 Estimated Unique Monthly Visitors
9. Infospace: 24,000,000 Estimated Unique Monthly Visitors
10. Info: 13,500,000 Estimated Unique Monthly Visitors
11. DuckDuckGo: 13,000,000 Estimated Unique Monthly Visitors

---

[4] http://www.ebizmba.com/articles/search-engines

12. Contenko: 11,000,000 Estimated Unique Monthly Visitors
13. Dogpile: 10,500,000 Estimated Unique Monthly Visitors
14. Alhea: 7,500,000 Estimated Unique Monthly Visitors
15. ixQuick: 4,000,000 Estimated Unique Monthly Visitors

In a 2015 study published on SearchEngineLand.com Eli Schwartz's research found the following breakdown of the users of search engines:

Search Engine	Market Share of Online Searches
Google	75%
Yahoo	8%
Bing	7%
DuckDuckGo	2%
AOL	1%
Ask	1%
Baidu	1%

Table 1 Search Engine Market Share Breakdown

According to InternetLiveStats.com there are **1.2 trillion searches per year** worldwide on Google.com. This means that there are 1,600,000,000,000 searches happening annually on the top seven search engines! Obtaining a fraction of the traffic from these extremely targeted prospects who are looking for your product or service is something that savvy business owners need for their company website. Depending on what your product price is, the value of 100 clients from 2,000 hits to your optimized website can be huge. This is money just on the table for your business to add to your bottom line.

This book focuses on the Google Search Engine because it has the largest slice of the search market traffic. Google has "smart" or "artificial intelligence" computers that work with big data gathered from those who interact on the internet. The data compiled looks at user intent and verbatim relevance to determine what results to show.

When you meet someone and they say "Google me" you know that search engines are in our vernacular and they are here to stay. For this reason, I wanted to talk about something we've all been taking for granted: The search engine itself. What is a search engine? How does a search engine work? How many people even think about this?

When I searched the question "What is a search engine" I found a lot of results, billions in fact. When I looked up the images I saw some pretty pictures, some really complicated diagrams and some not so much. As a result, I decided to explain it as I understand it from my own work experience.

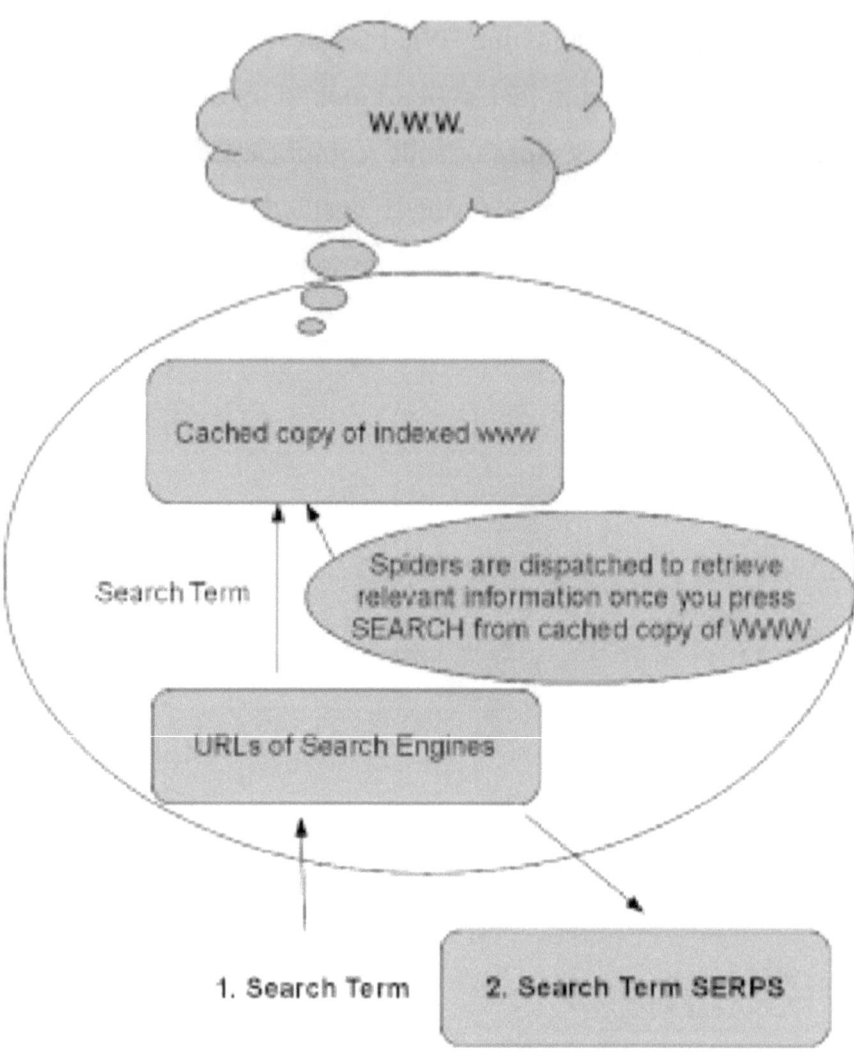

Figure 1 How does a Search Engine Work?

I like to think of search engines as a tool to organize data in a massive bucket. Without a search engine, jumping on the internet is hit and miss. All the data is jumbled up and it is not clear what goes where. However, when you put data in Google's Bucket, the bucket knows just how to organize the data so when you reach in to get the information that you have in mind you get it right away. When searching on Google you have to be specific. The data is organized or indexed into tables which are stored on servers or computers. You see this is very similar to the diagram of search engines above.

The World Wide Web is a conglomerate of Internet Service Providers all over the world that have servers/computers that lease space for data for websites to their customers. These customers make their websites public for the world to see. This is the raw data. The Search Engines have their websites and servers that have web applications, that we will call spiders that process commands to organize, request, store, and display this data at the user's pleasure.

Looking at the aforementioned Figure 1, the first step from the data consumer perspective is to think of a search term. Once the term is decided it is entered into the search box at the URL of the Search Engine of choice and then the fun begins.

Next the spiders receive the request and the cached copy of the internet that is most relevant is searched, identified, and ordered and then displayed (Search Engine Result Pages or SERPs) to the user in seconds in their browser where they made the original request. The user is not even looking at the actual copy of the owner's websites until they click the link. Cool huh?

This is how search engines work.

The goal of search engine optimization (SEO) is to make sure that your website is not stuck in the cloud anonymously, but you are known by your target audience. This is accomplished by developing relevant content, using the right keywords, and making sure that your website is in compliance with Google's Search Algorithms. These are search engine optimization strategies. Above all search engine optimization strategies that work, will get your site cached on your chosen search engine and target relevant keywords to get you your desired traffic. Finally Search Engines are a tool that can be used for your dream search term to make you noticed for your niche.

It is very important to understand the power of a search engine results page from every perspective. From the perspective of your target customer or prospect, it is the place where they will find the most relevant information that they are searching for. From a Digital Marketing Professional's perspective, it is the most desired digital real estate. From a Business branding perspective, this is the very first place where a potential customer will interact with your brand. In Table 2, you will see what percent of the total number of people searching on a specific keyword click on results 1-14.

Table 2 Traffic Percentage Breakdown

Google Result Page Rank	Average Traffic Share
1	32.5%
2	17.6%
3	11.4%
4	8.1%
5	6.1%

6	4.4%
7	3.5%
8	3.1%
9	2.6%
10	2.4%
11	1.0%
12	0.8%
13	0.7%
14	0.6%

Effective SEO is the best option with the highest return on investment out of any form of advertising. If your competitors keep ranking above you in the most popular search engines, you run the risk of being irrelevant.

With that said, it is important to understand that your Meta Title, Meta Description, and URL are the very first things that a potential client will see as they decide whether or not to visit your website. This is why keyword selection is extremely important. You want to make sure that your offerings and your website visitors intent are congruent. The next screenshot of Google's Search Engine Results page points out the location of the Meta Title, Meta Description, and URL on the Search Engine Results page.

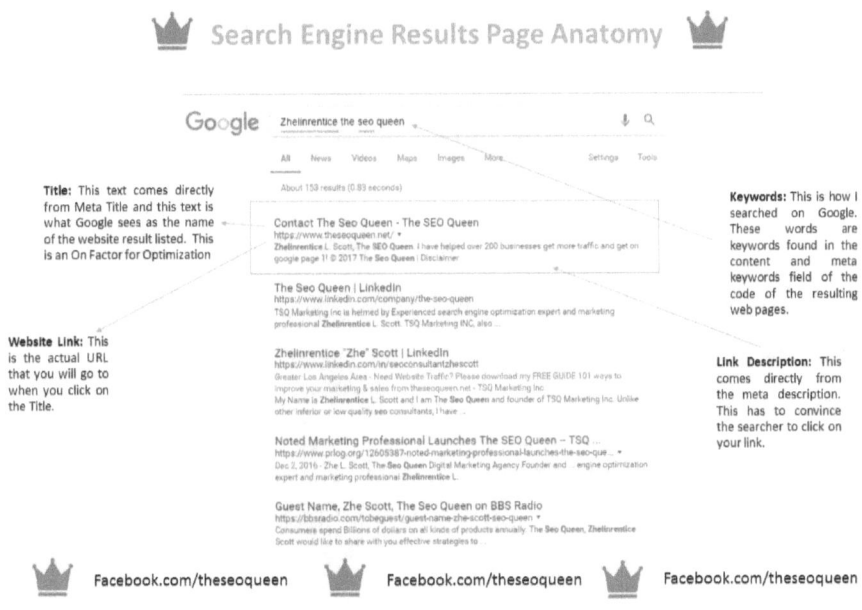

Figure 2 Anatomy of a Search Engine Results Page (SERPs)

Many Search Engine Optimization (SEO) Professionals, who are not a part of Google's corporation, debate the importance, and the merit of the use of keywords in digital marketing. Many SEO Professionals will tell you, as a business owner, that using keywords is not important. Some professionals believe that you should not worry about optimizing your alt tags, meta keywords, or including them in your content. I disagree. One thing that I know for sure is that keywords are the very foundation of a successful search engine optimization campaign. As you saw in the aforementioned screenshot of Google Search Results Page for the phrase "Zhe the seo queen" you see the keyword as the query into google, and the Meta Title is the text that is hyperlinked to the URL in the results. The Meta Description is the unclickable text underneath the hyperlinked Meta Title and URL. The Meta Description is the "billboard" for your link. It has to be interesting. The Meta Description is something that describes to the Google bots what they will find on your website. It has to be precise. It also has to be relevant and contain keywords. It is also the text that your potential website visitor will read before they decide to visit your website. Utilizing a call to action in your meta description is helpful and will increase your conversion rate from SERPs to your website.

 Go to www.google.com **and search for "search engines for RFPs". Do you see the URL, Meta Title,**

Meta Description in the results? What do you see? Who is on the first page? Ranked 1? 2? 3? 4? 5? What industry are you in? Search for your vertical's search engine and submit your website to that search engine.

Google SEO

What is important to Google? What is important to rank high on Google? One word: relevance.

I have had the opportunity of speaking with several employees of Google who work in various departments. Collectively they shed some light on what Google is looking for:

- **Relevant Meta Data:**

  Meta Data at the basic level consists of your Meta Title, Meta Description, and your Meta Keywords. These tags give Google and other search engines the information that they need to begin to understand the content on the website and how to serve that website to its users. The Meta Title and Description are very important as well to the search engine users because it is those tags that a user sees when a search engine results page appears. Relevance is also based on location, time, search history, topic, and device. When Google selects data to share with the users of its search engine, it will only serve data that it determines is relevant. For instance, if someone is searching for a plumber in New York they will not see the website of the plumber in California. Google's algorithms are smart enough to know which searches are local, national, or global in nature.

- **Incoming Links**

  Incoming Links to your website are important to Google and other search engines. Google counts these links like votes. Google's Algorithm looks at natural link growth as an indication of relevance to the internet community. The more popular, the more relevant, the more favorable Google will rank the site being linked to.

- **Relevant and Fresh Content**
  Google loves to give its users searching for information the best content available. Google loves to give rank to content that is shared on social media, linked to, emailed (to Gmail accounts), and has a very low bounce rate from those who view it. It is important to deliver value in your online content.

An inexpensive way to gain back links to your website is to have the following: Pinterest, Twitter, Blogger, etc. All of these websites you can post your URL as a back link to your site and drive up the popularity of your site.

Questions arise frequently about the pro and cons of having onsite of offsite Blog, the answer, straight from Google, that I heard was the following: it is better to have an off-site blog IF you are in need of back links. If you have an excellent back link strategy then an integrated blog is great for targeting long tailed keywords and creating fresh content.

Relevant and fresh content trumps all. Keyword density, reading level and all of that is nice, but at the end of the day does your website do the following:

- Is your content helpful and easy to understand?
- Contain your keywords?
- Is it constantly updated with fresh relevant material?
- Does it look natural?
- Does it have great website design?

In order to master Google SEO, your meta data, link building, and fresh content have to look natural. Going to extremes will get you penalized.

Do you have a website that you want to optimize? If you do not have an existing website, pause now and start your website. You will get much more out of this book if you have a website that you can optimize. If you are not sure what platform or website content management system to use, go to wix.com and create a site. You will be able to practice on that platform until you can purchase a domain and launch your website using WordPress or another professional content management platform.

Keyword Research: How Your Ideal Prospects Find You

It's interesting...

Did you know that your website can rank for Keyphrases that you are not even aiming for?

The purpose of this chapter is to clarify the language used when referring to keywords and how to find the best keywords.

What are Keywords?

Keywords, or what I also like to call Keyphrases, are the foundation of a successful search engine optimization campaign. Keywords are the way by which prospective customers, fans, or businesses will find you from a search on a search engine.

Keywords can consist of 1, 2, 3, 4, or 5 individual words.

How Can I Pick the Best Keywords?

For example, let's consider how a potential customer would search for a poodle to buy.

The top ways that people search to buy a poodle are:

Keyword used by potential dog owners	Monthly Searches on Google.com

poodle	301,000
poodle dog	14,800
toy poodle puppies	6,600
teacup poodle dogs for sale	20
poodle dog pure bred	0
teacup poodle dogs for sale	0

Table 3 Top Poodle Searches via Google Keyword Tool in 2015

As you can see here there is a pattern. One-word Keyphrases get a lot of traffic. This is how people who are looking to purchase a poodle are searching.

As an owner of a small business or employee that is looking to increase the amount of internet visibility for your company's website this has to be understood. One-word phrases tend to have more search volume and much more competition than the longer Keyphrases.

The best strategy for picking the best Keyphrases is simple. Pick the keywords with the most search volume and the least amount of competition. The longer the Keyphrase the lower the amount of traffic. However, the shorter the Keyphrase, the tougher and longer it will take to rank. The longer the Keyphrase the easier and faster it is rank.

There are ways to automate this research, but I think that it is very important for you as a part of a small business organization to understand the nuances of keyword research.

You can pick the best keywords through meticulous analysis of the content on your website. You can also identify the best keywords for your campaign through anecdotal and quantitative analysis.

When you are trying to take your website to the next level, but are not sure about where to start, analyze the phrases within your existing content for inspiration. There are tools that can automate this process for you, but you can do this yourself simply by reading every page
on your website again, and writing down a list of phrases that pop out at you.

After you have done this talk to your customers, staff and colleagues to determine what language is being used to describe your product or service. Continue to add this information to your list.

Once you have your preliminary list to examine, now it is time for the quantitative analysis of your keywords.

Using Keyword Research Tools and Strategies:

You can go to Google's Keyword Planner located here:
https://adwords.google.com/ko/KeywordPlanner/Home

The keyword tool can give you search volume, Cost per Click, targeted search volume by geography, and device search volume as well. Please note that you can pull search volumes by the world, country, state, county, and city.

If you want to know how many people in the state of Nebraska are searching to buy a poodle from their mobile devices you can find that number using this tool.

With the location based search volume in your hands for every possible way that your potential customers are searching for you, you can now look at the competition levels for each phrase.

Please note that Google Keyword Tool gives you a metric called competition that goes from 0 to 1. This is simply based on how competitive the phrase is with respect to paid ads.

Make sure you have a Gmail account created. That is the best way to access Google Interfaces like Google Keyword Tool. Please visit this link:
https://adwords.google.com/ko/KeywordPlanner/Home/.
You will only be able to access this link when you log into Google via your Gmail credentials. Once you land on the page then put in 10 phrases, (where there is a circle) that come to mind when describing your product or service. You have entered your "seed keywords", when you search you will see what related Keyphrases Google is selling ads for. This data is helpful when planning an organic search campaign.

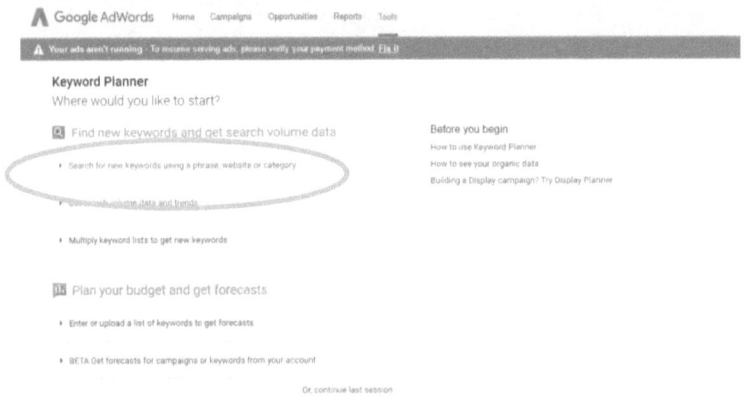

Figure 3 Google Keyword Tool Interface Screenshot 2015

When you want to determine how much search engine optimization competition a phrase has, you want to go to google.com and you want to put in the phrase in yourself and search on it.

When you take the word "poodle" and put the phrase in to google.com you will see the SERP or the Search Engine Results Page appear.

It looks like this:

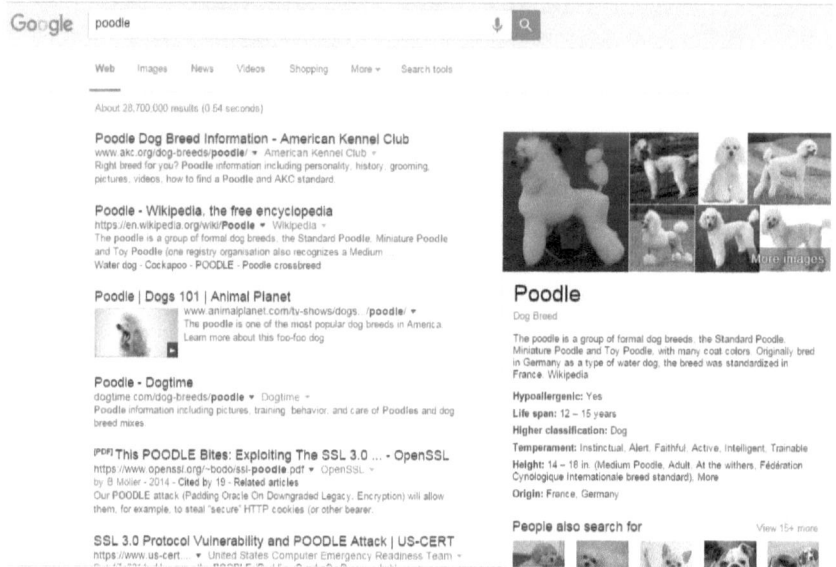

Figure 4 Screenshot of 2015 Google Search for phrase "Poodle"

As you can see, there is the number 28,700,000 on the page. This number means that 28.7 million websites are ranking for the word poodle. This may seem like a lot; however, you want to know how many people are looking to get traffic on the word "poodle" specifically. You can dig deeper and find that number by going to google.com and putting the following in to the google.com search box: allintitle: poodle

It looks like this:

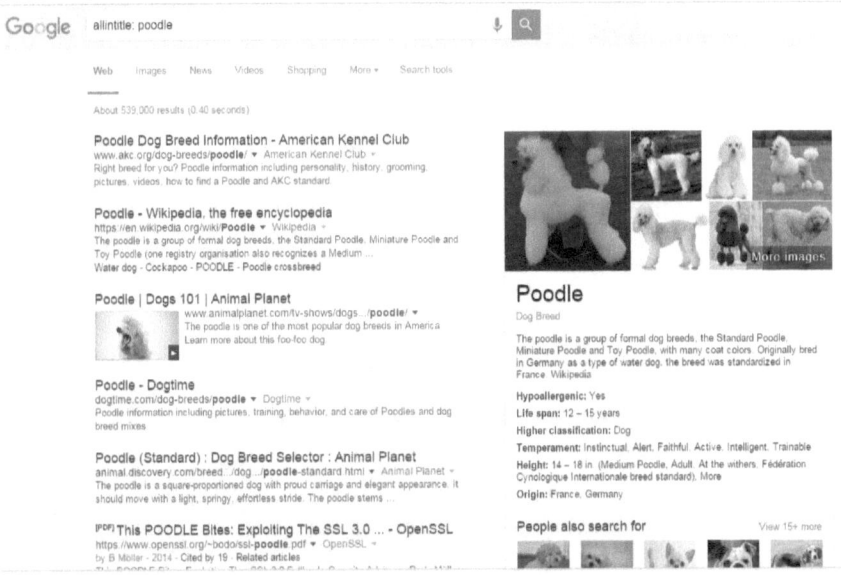

Figure 5 Screenshot of Google 2015 query for allintitle: poodle

As you can see here, the number has been reduced dramatically. It is now 539,000. This number is the number of pages that have the word "poodle" in the meta title of the website in Google's index. This is dramatically less than 28.7 million, but it is still competitive. To rank on page 1 for this phrase you will need the following:

- *Thousands of pages of content indexed by google about poodles.*
- *Thousands of quality backlinks.*

This is definitely a daunting reality for any small business entrepreneur or employee.

Now, let's look at the phrase "toy poodle puppies". When you look at the entire Google index for this phrase you find that 1.3 million websites are ranking for this term. When you search on this term like this: **allintitle: toy poodle puppies** you will see that 33,500 websites have the phrase "toy poodle puppies" in their meta title tag. This is an average amount of competition.

When you find a phrase with thousands of hits per month and less than 50,000 pages with that word in the title, this is a high traffic, average competition phrase. Phrases where less than 1,000 websites are targeting the phrase in the meta title are an immediate addition to my organic search engine optimization campaign if the user intent on Google page 1 is in agreement with my business objectives.

If you are having a hard time finding a keyword that gets great traffic with low competition, Google Suggest can also help you find keywords for your campaign.

WHAT IS GOOGLE SUGGEST?

Google Suggest is Google's way of helping users save time by giving them suggestions as they type.

See:

Figure 6 Screenshot of 2015 Google Query "allintitle: toy poodle puppies"

This is where the keyword strategy is essential for success. If your analysis has not yielded enough feasible ideas for your search engine optimization campaign, using Google suggest can give you long tailed keywords that will convert. Long Tailed Keywords is the fancy term for keyword phrases with 3 or more words in them.

Google Suggests the following phrases for Toy Poodle Puppies:

>Toy poodle puppies for sale
>Toy poodle puppies information

Toy poodle puppies for adoption
Toy poodles for sale
Toy poodle breeders
Toy poodle information
Toy poodle rescue
Toy poodles for adoption

Now, using the new-found familiarity with Google's Keyword Tool you can put those phrases in to the que and get the search volume[5].

Keyword used by potential dog owners	Monthly Searches on Google.com
toy poodles for sale	9,900
toy poodle puppies	6,600
toy poodle puppies for sale	4,400
toy poodle rescue	1,900
toy poodle breeders	1,600
toy poodles for adoption	480
toy poodle information	390
toy poodle puppies for adoption	110
toy poodle puppies information	90

Table 4 Google Keyword Tool Search Volume Results 2015

The keyword that pops out at me is: ***toy poodle puppies for sale***

---

[5] Please Note that Google has changed the data available in the Free Google Keyword Tools to ranges instead of exact numbers.

This phrase pops out at me as a viable addition to the campaign because it has 5 words. This is the best length for long tailed keywords, because it will fit into the Meta Title guidelines perfectly with no additional wordsmithing required. To optimize a page further with this keyword, I would include it in the content 1-3 times in the page text that would total 500-900 words on that page. I would also include that phrase in the meta description as well.

Now let's see what the competition on this phrase looks like. Let's search Google normally, and there are approximately 1.7 million results. Now let's see how many pages in Google's index are actually targeting this phrase through Keyphrase placement in their web page title: 16,300 pages are targeting this phrase.

16,300 is perfect when you consider that this phrase "toy poodle puppies for sale" gets 4,400 searches per month on average. The Ideal level of competition is less than 100,000 websites aiming for that phrase. I personally love when I find phrases that have less than a hundred thousand web pages targeting that phrase. In this case, getting rank for "toy poodle puppies for sale" is relatively quick.

 **Go to** www.google.com **and search using one of your "seed keywords" that you used earlier. As you are typing the phrase in, notice what phrases that Google suggests as you type. Write those phrases down, and go back to the Google Search Tool and enter the phrases revealed by Google Suggest. Make a note of the search volume is like for those keywords. Here is the link to Google's Keyword Tool for your reference:**
https://adwords.google.com/ko/KeywordPlanner/Home/

The Difference between Short Tail and Long Tail Keywords

Short Tail keywords typically have more traffic and incredibly high competition. Short tailed phrases like: dress, shoes, chair, table have a ton of competition because it is a simple and obvious phrase that immediately comes to mind when a person is searching for something on the
internet. Viable Long Tailed Keywords usually take more research time to discover. The reason that this process often takes more time, is because checking the search volume is quick, but
using the google.com operator allintitle, takes time. The time spent is worth it!

No business owner wants to try to rank on Google page 1 for a phrase that is extremely competitive if it takes over a year. Most business owners need results as quickly as possible.

In depth: Search Volume

The following image is a screenshot of Google's AdWords Tool. The Google AdWords Tool takes the data from 12 previous months and gives you the average search volume of searches on Google's search engine in the country, state, or city that you specify. This tool is ideal for estimating the impact of a google page 1 ranking for a specific keyword. If you look at the phrase "toy poodles for sale" you will see that the Search Volume is 9,900 searches per month on average.

Figure 7 Google Keyword Tool Comparison 2015

In depth: Competition Level

Search Operator Code:	What results it Gives
Allintitle:	Gives you the number of websites that have that keyword phrase in their Meta Title
Allinurl:	Gives you the number of websites that have that keyword phrase in their URL.
Site:	Gives you all of the pages that are being indexed on your website on google
Link:	Gives you the number and the exact links that your site has to it. It is a great way to look at a snap shot of your backlinks.

Table 5 Google Operators that work in 2017

The next figures give you a snap shot of the google search operators in action. I have included screenshots of the phrases poodle, toy poodle puppies, and toy poodle puppies for sale. Please note that the number of websites or competition decreases with the length of the keyword phrase.

The next screenshot is of the results for the following command:

Allintitle: poodle

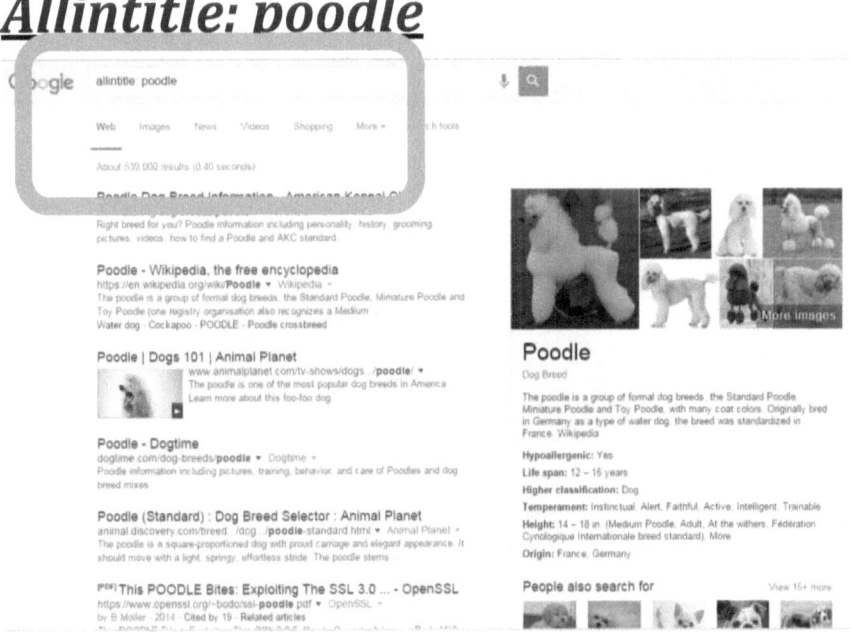

Figure 8 Screenshot of 2015 results for allintitle: poodle

The next screenshot is of the results for the following command:

Allintitle: toy poodle puppies

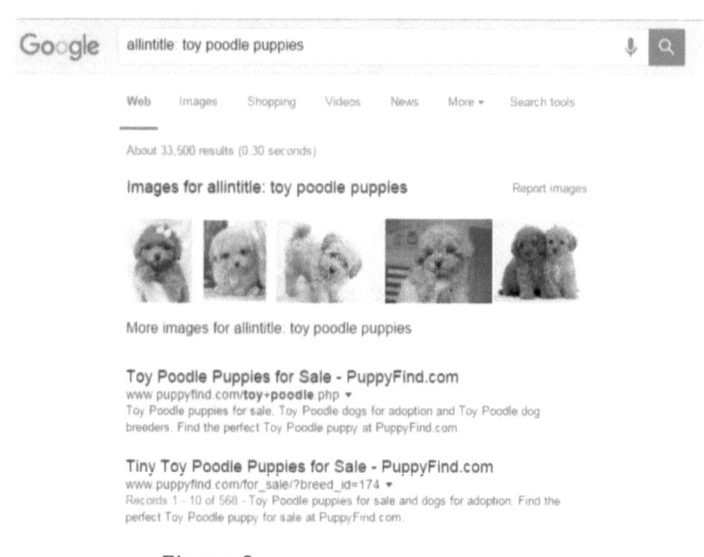

Figure 9

The next screenshot is of the results for the following command:

Allintitle: toy poodle puppies for sale

Google   allintitle: toy poodle puppies for sale

Web Shopping Images Videos News More ▼ Search tools

About 16,300 results (0.33 seconds)

Toy Poodle Breeder & AKC Puppies for Sale Los Angeles ...
redandapricot**poodle**s.com/ ▼
Scarlet's Fancy Poodles is an AKC registered breeder offering Toy Apricot & Red Poodle Puppies for Sale near Los Angeles & San Francisco, California –

toy poodle Dogs & puppies For Sale in Los Angeles| eBay ...
losangeles.ebayclassifieds.com › All ads › Pets › Dogs & puppies ▼ Kijiji ▼
Find toy poodle Dogs & puppies for sale: terriers, labradors, blue nose & other dogs for sale in Los Angeles. Best free local ads from eBay Classifieds - Page 1

Images for allintitle: toy poodle puppies for sale   Report images

More images for allintitle: toy poodle puppies for sale

Tiny Toy Poodle Puppies for Sale - PuppyFind.com
www.puppyfind.com/**for_sale**/?breed_id=174 ▼
Records 1 - 10 of 568 - Toy Poodle puppies for sale and dogs for adoption. Find the perfect Toy Poodle puppy for sale at PuppyFind.com.

Toy Poodle Puppies for Sale - PuppyFind.com
www.puppyfind.com/**toy+poodle**.php ▼
Toy Poodle puppies for sale, Toy Poodle dogs for adoption and Toy Poodle dog breeders. Find the perfect Toy Poodle puppy at PuppyFind.com.

The next screenshot is of the results for the following command:

Allinurl: toy poodle puppies for sale

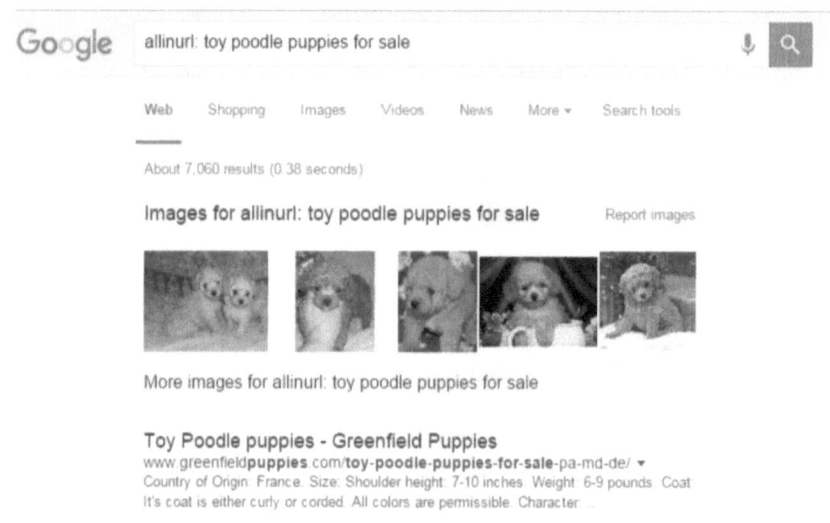

There are only 7,060 results. This lets me know that the URL has to include the new long tailed keyword phrase that we are adding to the campaign. This is easy to do if you have a site in development, however if you are needing to add content to your site to rank for a certain phrase, I would create the page and make sure that the URL uses hyphens and includes the phrase that I am targeting for my SEO Campaign. Please note that underscores in a URL is not in compliance with Google's Search Algorithm.

KEYWORD PLACEMENT CONSIDERATIONS:

When you are determining whether or not a keyword is relevant for the customers who intend to find you, just visit google page 1 for that term that you are considering. When you see the Search Engine Results Page or SERPs, please ask yourself, is this page targeted to the types of people who want my services? Is it intuitively obvious?

If the answer is yes that people are looking for what you offer on google page 1, then that phrase is a good choice. Another great question to ask yourself is about user intent AND branding: Does this SERP page embarrass or misrepresent my brand? If the answer is no to that question, then the keyword in question is a GREAT keyword discovery for you that should be included. If the "neighbors" that you would be found among would tarnish your brand, then that keyword is obviously not a good fit. These questions are very important because they will prevent any negative views of your brand, and eliminate the possibility of a high bounce rate. Bounce rate is the percent of people who visit your website that leave immediately. If you have a high percentage 50-80%, depending on your niche, this can negatively affect your ability to rank for more keywords over time. Google's algorithm does appreciate a low bounce rate because a low bounce rate insures that the quality of content is very good for the users who arrive to your website via the term it is ranking for. The great thing about Google is that your website can target low competition phrases with the right user intent in a great neighborhood. In a great neighborhood on Google Page 1, your company website traffic will thrive.

Not to beat a dead horse, but if you chose the wrong keyword(s) this can damage your brand in a few ways. Prospects will create a sky-high bounce rate for you and diminish your ability to rank for additional keywords because the trust and authority of your site will be stagnated.

Please remember that Content is King for Google. Also remember that User Experience and User Intent are equally important. If your users cannot find what they thought you had by reading your title and meta description in the Google SERP, then they will leave in a few seconds, cause you to have a high bounce rate and hinder your ability to improve your keyword placement.

Finally ask yourself: Will the people searching on that keyword find what they are looking for? Will your website appearance in the SERPs matter to them? Are you and your brand comfortable with appearing on Google page 1 in that neighborhood?

Please go to Use Google Suggest: type in a phrase that you think people are search for you by, write down the suggested phrases that pop up as you type, Write down the suggested phrases at the bottom of the SERP. Please note: I like to take screen shots as the results pop up so that I will not miss a phrase. Checklist: Have you picked keyword phrases that are 2-4 words in length? Have you checked google page 1 for the targeted keywords and confirmed that the user intent is in line with your desired customer's needs? Have you picked keywords that have a decent search volume?

On-Page Implementation Success

An effective website has to have the right content, contact information, call to action, and be in compliance with Google's Algorithms. My philosophy in approaching Google is to leverage the Google Algorithms as much as possible. I like for my websites to be mobile friendly, heavy with 500-900 words of content per page. I like all of my images to be optimized with alt tags. Finally, I like to leverage Schema markup and Meta Data. All of those factors affect your website's level of Google Compliance and overall visibility online. All of your website pages require on page optimization. As a business owner, the aforementioned factors have to be optimized with consideration for your content organization, brand, website content management system, and many other things that affect your choice on how your present your company online.

Since Google is looking at so many factors, a business owner can pick and choose which ones to get into compliance. I think the low hanging fruit or the factors that are fairly easy to control for a business owner for On Page Implementation are the following:

- Word Count
- Keyword Use
- Meta Data
- HTML Code
- Website Design over all
- Page Loading Speed
- Images
- URL

Digging deeper into Google's Panda, Penguin, Hummingbird, and Mobile Algorithms, research shows that there are 200 factors that determine how Google will rank your website within its search engine results. The Panda Algorithm eliminates any search results that have poor quality or plagiarized on page content. The Penguin Algorithm update eliminates high ranks for websites that have links from link farms and low-quality sites. The Hummingbird algorithm update gives better keyword rankings to content that answers popular questions. The Mobile Algorithm gives preference to websites that are mobile friendly and mobile optimized. All of these algorithms can be confusing. This is why I love infographics to explain tough concepts. The next infographic groups factors by on and off page, content, links, and more. Search Engine Land created this powerful infographic, it helps me, and I know that it will help you. Over 200 factors are organized simplify complex search engine optimization strategies. Here is Search Engine Land's Info graphic called: The Periodic Table of SEO Success Factors:

You can learn more about this graphic by visiting http://searchengineland.com/seotable.

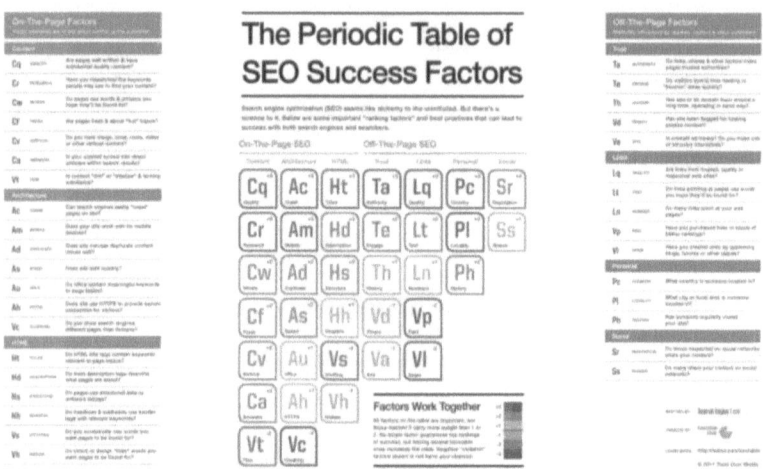

Figure 10 Periodic Table of SEO Success Factors

As a business owner, one simple thing that you can do to improve your search engine results and keyword placement is to make sure that every page has a minimum word count between 500 and 900 words with a sensible keyword density. A natural keyword density is 2-6% depending on the length, purpose, and quality of the content. It has to make sense to the average website visitor to avoid penalties from Google.

Keyword density = (# of times the targeted Keyphrase appears)/Total number of words.

One rule of thumb is to avoid high keyword density. Any keyword density in the double digits runs the risk of looking like keyword stuffing to Google and prompting penalties. Ideally, you want your content to look as natural as possible. You can use synonyms for your target keywords and that will help. Utilize synonyms with search volume on Google. Once you have identified your desired keywords, it is often very useful to determine what 3-5 keyword phrases should appear on each page, and you should aim to include each of your targeted phrases for that page a minimum of 1 time on that page.

Please remember that Google is in the business of serving content to visitors. The higher the quality of the content the higher it will rank. If your content answers a popular question, and uses the h1, h2, and h3 tags to organize the content, Google loves that, and in some cases, has awarded a gift in the knowledge graph. The more content or words that you have on a page, the more favorably Google will rank your content. The bottom line is that each page within your site should have as much high-quality content as possible. Other things that should appear on each page of your website are:

- ✓ 1 H1 Tag that contains your targeted Keyphrase. The H1 Tag cannot be the same as your Meta Title.
- ✓ The first paragraph of your content should contain your keyword
- ✓ Your content should have a unique image
- ✓ Your content should have a relevant video imbedded

as well.
- ✓ Each image should have a unique alt tag as well.

META DATA:

The Meta Data of your webpage is very important. Again, your meta data is the first way that prospects will encounter your company. The next diagram describes which part of the results on Google Page 1 belong to each type of Meta Data.

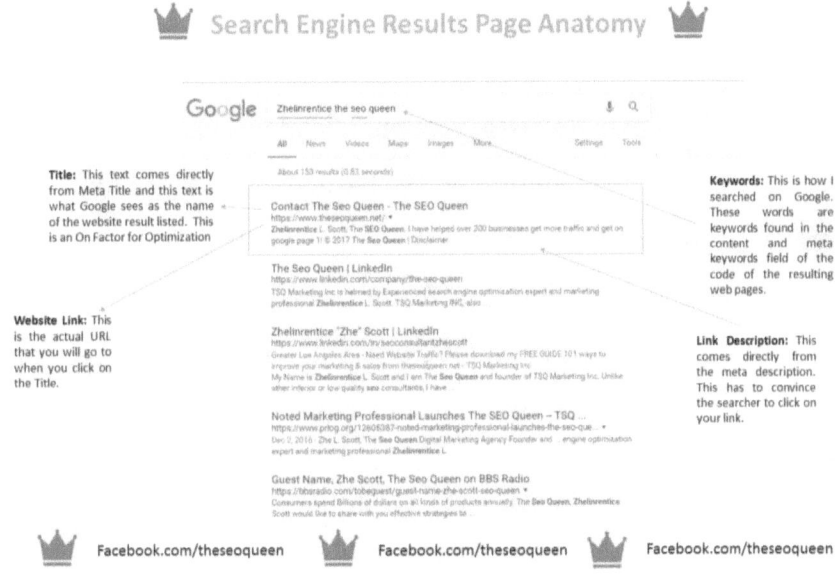

Figure 11 Search Engine Results Page Anatomy

Figure 11 shows that the Meta Title and Meta Description are the text that Google shows the user along with your URL. The purpose of the Meta Data is twofold. The first purpose is to make it clear to Google that your website is relevant for your targeted Keyphrases. The second purpose is to convince potential prospects to investigate your company because they feel that you will meet the requirements for the product or service that they are looking for. Your Meta Title and Meta Description must spur people to action to click through to your website.

To Optimize your Meta Data, you must remember that the **Meta Title** can only be a maximum of 55 characters in length and your Meta Description can only be a maximum of 150 characters. To optimize your meta title your Keyphrase must be at the very beginning of the text string. For instance, for the phrase, "toy poodles for sale", a great title tag looks like:

<title> Toy Poodles For Sale | Toy Poodle Puppies Information </title>

I am using 2 phrases that have 9,900 and 90 hits respectively. The title tag is total of 53 characters long. This title tag is 2 characters short of the 55 maximum that Google will display, and it is not too short. This is optimal. Two related phrases in my title tag. Yay!

 Using the Keywords that you identified previously use them to construct title and description for a page within your site. Please use the Google Snippet Optimizer to guide your efforts the link is here: http://snippetoptimizer.net/google-serp/

BODY TEXT:

The body text is what prospects will see in their web browsers once they land on your website. The "body text" view of your website excludes html links, video, images, and other multimedia. This unclickable text is what Google loves. The more unclickable text you have, the more phrases Google can index you for. Again, unclickable text should have your Keyphrase appear a minimum of 1 time. Your Keyphrase density should be 2 to 6%, and your word count should be 500-900 words. A Bonus tip: An easy way to keep your keyword density to an acceptable level is to adopt this rule of thumb: no more than 3 instances of your phrase for every 300 words. Also, enhance the SEO Power of your website through the use synonyms in your text. This will avoid black hat keyword stuffing and leverage the value that the Hummingbird Google Algorithm gives for rich content.

H1 Headline Text:

Headline or H1 Tags enclose text between the <h1> and </h1> tags in the html code. Please go to your website and right click. Select: View Source and search the code there for the text string: "h1". Your Headline text should contain your Keyphrase. For example:

<h1> Toy Poodles For Sale </h1>

H2-H6 HEADLINE TEXT:

Since the roll out of the Google's Hummingbird Algorithm, I have noticed that pages fully optimized to answer a user's question using H2-H6 tags to format not only get the first rank, but their content can appear on the SERP as a part of the Knowledge Graph. The Knowledge Graph "is more about providing richer answers directly in the search results, often answering the user's questions directly without her having to click through to a website."[6]. This is huge. For a business owner that has the question as the title with a <h1> tag and then numbers each item in the list with the <h2> tag, you can get some pretty good placement. The next screenshots show in detail how the following knowledge graph result was achieved. This is important information to consider because you can use this exact approach to go after Knowledge Graph visibility.

---

[6] Eric Enge, Stephan Spencer, and Jessie C. Stricchiola, *Art Of SEO* (O'Reilly Media, Inc, 2015) p. 64

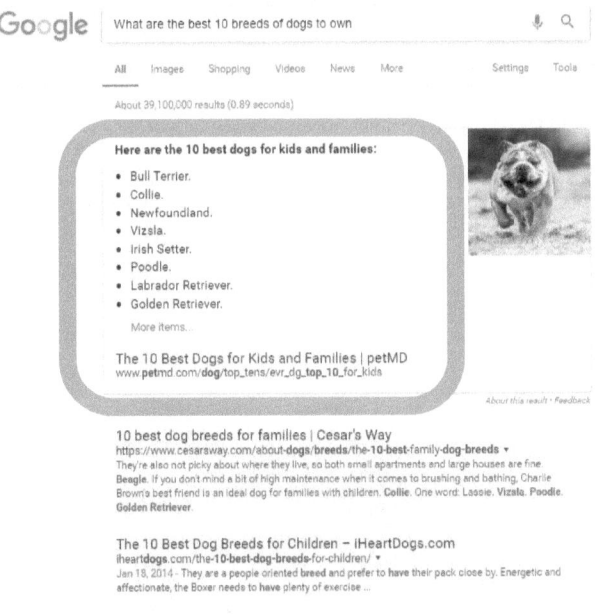

Figure 12 Knowledge Graph in the SERP

As you can see here, the list from the website PETMD.com has a result in the knowledge graph. I searched on the phrase "What are the best 10 breeds of dogs to own". When you look at the code on the page: http://www.petmd.com/dog/top_tens/evr_dg_top_10_for_kids the code reveals that the H1 tag is there. This result was achieved through the use of the <ul> list tag with bullets <li>. An example of the code format is as follows:

```
<!DOCTYPE html>
<html>
<body>

<h1>Please Visit the Following Webpages</h1>

<ul>
  <li><a href="Ladyzhe.com">Ladyzhe.com</a></li>
  <li><a href="TheSeoqueen.net">TheSeoqueen.net</a>
  </li>
  <li><a href="TSQMarketing.com">TSQMarketing.com</a>
  </li>
</ul>

</body>
</html>
```

Please Visit the Following Webpages

- Ladyzhe.com
- TheSeoqueen.net
- TSQMarketing.com

Figure 13 Code Example for Hummingbird Formatting

The previous screenshot[7] shows a list of 3 websites. This code is the same approach used in the PetMD website. This is an example of the code strategy used on PetMD to get the knowledge graph entry on the search engine results page. Now we are going to move from just the H1 tag and the Bulleted lists in to incorporating H2, H3, and H4.

To show you how websites have leveraged the Hummingbird Algorithm and gotten additional visibility using the knowledge graph, I did a Google Search on the phrase: "How to Install a Light bulb."

The following screenshot shows you the results of that query:

---

[7] W3Schools (1997-2017). HTML Lists. Retrieved from https://www.w3schools.com/html/tryit.asp?filename=tryhtml_lists_unordered

Figure 14 Knowledge Graph Result for A Popular Question

At the time of the writing of this book, Homeserve.com is the website that has the top spot and a knowledge graph result. The URL with the top result is:

https://www.homeserve.com/help-advice/electrical/how-to-change-a-light-bulb.aspx.

This page is fully optimized for this Keyphrase. It is important to note that the URL contains the Keyphrase "How to Install a Light bulb". Now, looking at the code of the page here:

view-source:https://www.homeserve.com/help-advice/electrical/how-to-change-a-light-bulb.aspx

I see that the H1, H2, and H3 tags are used strategically. This next screenshot uses inspect element to show the H1 tag on the phrase "How to Change a light bulb". There is an arrow from the code to the content on the live, customer facing web page.

Figure 15 Code Reveal for HomeServe.com page answering a popular question

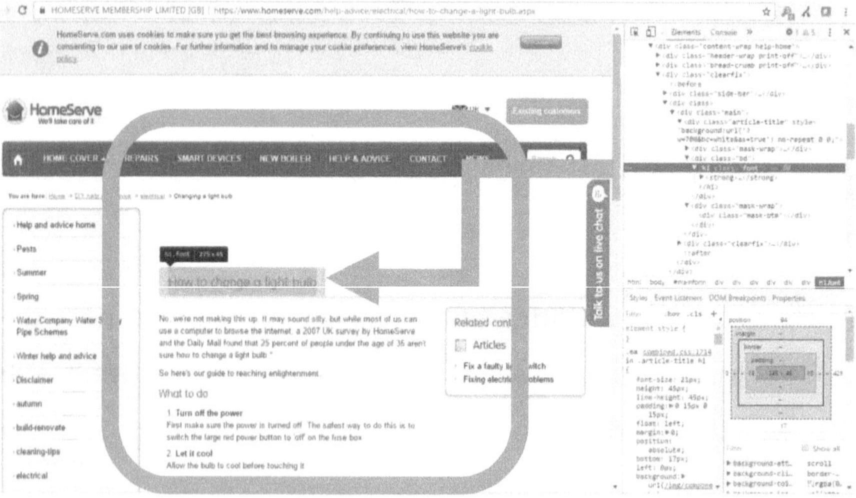

After the H1 Tag, an introduction using regular body text formatting comes next. After the introduction formatted as normal body text, the subheading of "What to do" is next. This is formatted with the H2 tag. The screen shot of this code is next. Again, there is an arrow from the code to the content on the live, customer facing web page.

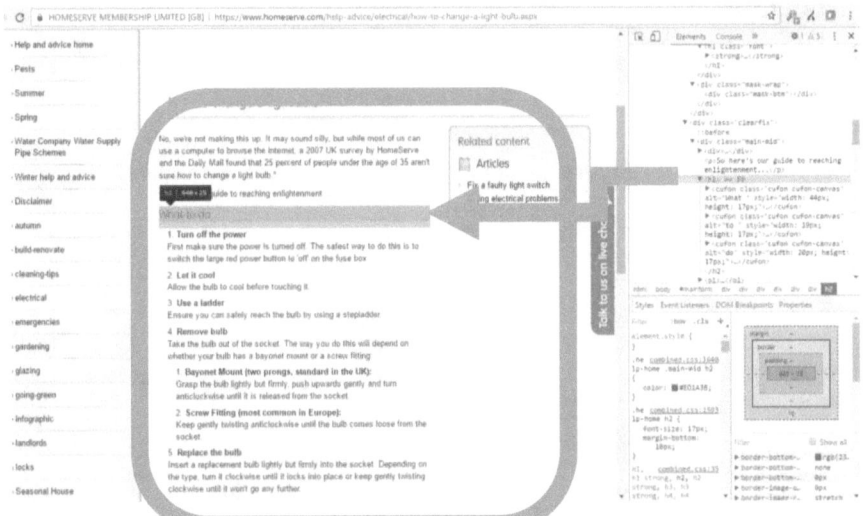

Figure 16 Code Reveal for <h2> tag use

On this page, the H2 tag has the text "What to Do" I see that the H1, H2, and H3 tags are used strategically. Next the list of steps to light bulb installation is formatted step by step via the HTML for a list. This code is similar to the code seen earlier in Figure 13. Here it is for a recap:

```html
<!DOCTYPE html>
<html>
<body>

<h1>Please Visit the Following Webpages</h1>

<ul>
  <li><a href="Ladyzhe.com">Ladyzhe.com</a></li>
  <li><a href="TheSeoqueen.net">TheSeoqueen.net</a></li>
  <li><a href="TSQMarketing.com">TSQMarketing.com</a></li>
</ul>

</body>
</html>
```

Please Visit the Following Webpages

- Ladyzhe.com
- TheSeoqueen.net
- TSQMarketing.com

The following screen shot shows the HTML code used on www.homeserve.com where they listed the steps of lightbulb installation.

Figure 17 Code reveal of the HTML for the list

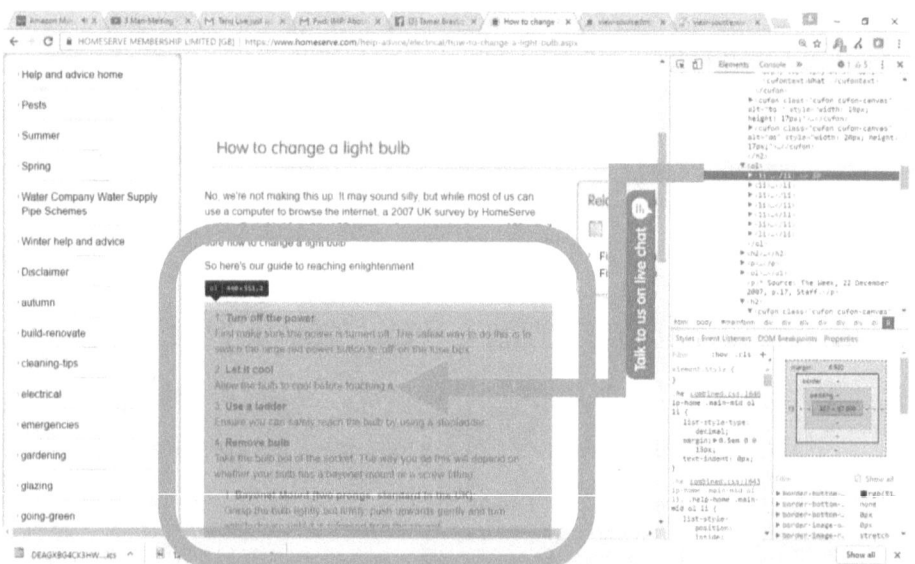

 Go to siteliner.com, run an analysis of your website. Look at your overview report, and take note of all of the pages that have a word count under 300 words. Create a content plan to get each page with thin content to 500-900 words employing the H1, H2, H3 formatting strategy whenever possible.

DOMAIN NAME AND URL OPTIMIZATION

If you are a business owner who has not committed to a certain domain name publicly you should consider buying a domain that contains one of the keyword phrases that you are targeting. For instance, a great domain name for the keyword phrase: "Toy Poodles For Sale"

Would be:

ToyPoodlesForSale.com
ToyPoodesForSale.net
ToyPoodlesForSale.biz
ToyPoodlesForSale.co

If you have to choose between a .com, .net, .biz, or .co domain name selecting .com is the most favorable. However, if a domain name you want is already taken, it is helpful to use .net, .biz, or co. There is nothing wrong with that. All of those aforementioned suffixes will rank.

KEYWORDS AND IMAGES:

Your keyword research is also valuable when it comes to your website images. Every image on your website should have Alt Text. Alt text website code looks like:

<img   src="companylogo.jpg"   width="300"   height="100" alt="Keyphrase describing picture">

Your image file name should also contain either your company name, a Keyphrase, or both.

You can also use Picasa (www.google.com/picasa) to insert your address into your images for maximum reach with your images. Please note that the ideal length for an alt tag is a maximum of 100 characters. The best practices for image optimization is the following:

1. Name your image using accurate keywords and descriptive terms.
2. Be as descriptive as you can with your alt tag. In the case of our poodles, "poodle puppy" is less desirable than "toy poodle puppy for sale" as an alt tag. This is because the longer phrase has more information.

For additional insight on the best approach to alt tags please refer to Google's alt tag guidelines here: https://support.google.com/webmasters/answer/114016?hl=en

Finally:

Please make sure that every page within your site has a Meta Title, Meta Description, Meta Keywords, and a word count 500-900 words for best results. You often hear that less is more, but more is more in the world of SEO page content. Content is King.

 **Go to Your website, install the SEO Site Tools plugin into your Google Chrome Browser. This plugin was mentioned in the productivity tools at the beginning of this book (Carter Cole's SEO Site Tools Chrome Plugin http://blog.cartercole.com/2010/02/seo-site-tools-chrome-seo-extension.html), and look at its analysis of 5 important pages on your site. Take note of all of the pages that do not have a Meta Title, a Meta Description, or Meta Keywords. Start writing your new meta tags using this tool: http://snippetoptimizer.net/google-serp/**

Off Page Implementation Success

In the On-Page Optimization section, we discussed optimizing the text, html, coding, meta data, images, and other media. Optimizing the code of the website is a very necessary step in the journey to Google Page 1, however there are off page factors that can be optimized for your website's benefit. Off Page Optimization is important to improve keyword placement. This section discusses in detail the factors that are not on the pages of your website that affect your company website keyword placement. The Off-Page Implementation process plays a major role in getting your company website ranked for extremely competitive terms. A properly executed off page campaign will avoid penalties and it will improve your campaign's keyword placement.

BACKLINKS

If you are a new to the world of SEO, you may or may not have heard of Backlinks.

What is a backlink? What is a backlink good for? What type of backlink is good? A Backlink is a hyperlink to your website from another website. The anchor text is the text that you see highlighted that the site visitor can click to travel to your website from the site with the link. At the very least as a Business Owner, you always want to get trusted and useful websites linking to yours. Related industry trade organizations, complementary products and services, chambers of commerce, trade publication websites, active business forums, and local/national business directories are ALL great places to acquire backlinks from.

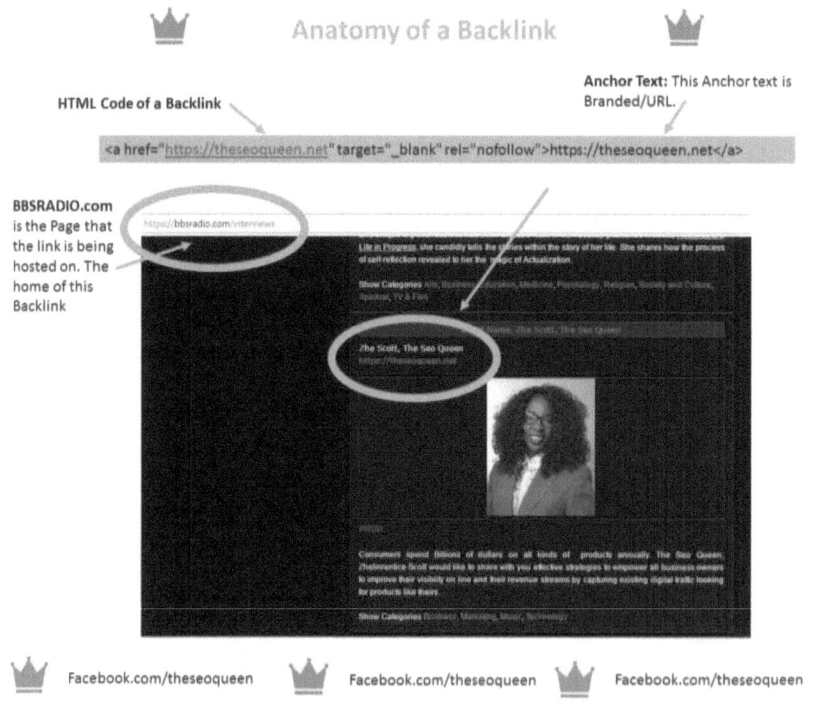

Figure 18 Anatomy of a Backlink

The aforementioned diagram is a screenshot of one of my backlinks to www.theseoqueen.net. I have highlighted the html and identified key parts of the code. The Anchor Text, is the URL https://theseoqueen.net. You can see that in purple, and it is circled in gold on the webpage screen shot above. The page that the anchor text is linking to is highlighted in the gold, that URL is the same as the anchor text. This is important to understand a backlink is simply a hyper link from another website to yours.

When you are building backlinks please make sure that you are optimizing your entire backlink profile. you want the anchor text to be either your URL/Company/ Brand Name; generic phrase such as "visit this website, for more information, or click here"; or a Keyphrase. A good rule of thumb is to have 1/3 of the anchor text to be the target URL, Company or Brand Name. 1/3 of the anchor text consist of generic phrases such as "website" "click here", "for more information". The final 1/3 should consist of your target keyword phrases and variations of those keywords. This is the ideal mix for a very natural looking back link profile for a website. What you want to avoid is looking completely over optimized by having 100% of the anchor text of your backlinks be all keywords. You can use tools such as Market Samurai and Majestic.com to evaluate your backlink profile and see what your anchor text mix is.

Create a free account on majestic.com. Do a search on your URL. Scroll down and you will see a pie chart for the anchor text mix for your website. Do you have any backlinks? Is the Anchor text all keywords? Do you have a mix? Do you have a 1/3 Brand and URL? 1/3 Generic phrases? 1/3 Keyword phrases?

BACKLINK SOURCES:

Some Great sources of quality backlinks can either be found or created on the following sites:

- Wordpress.com
- YouTube
- Medium

- Hub pages
- WIX
- Pinterest

- Weebly
- Snitz
- LinkedIn Publishing

- Google Forum Search
- Backlink Magic

- Google BlogSpot
- Yahoo Answers Closed Questions

- Follow Blog
- phpBB.com

- Yahoo Answers Open Questions

- Vbulletin

To recap, Backlinks can be procured from the following sources:

1. Business Directories
2. Complementary businesses
3. Trade Associations
4. Business Affiliations
5. SEO Press Releases

Takeaway: Make a list of 20 websites that you can ask the website owners to link to your website with either your company name or your URL as the hyperlinked text.

Social Media: The Essential Social Profiles

Social Media Marketing is very important to generate both referral traffic and improved keyword placement. Social Media is very important to Google, and this is evidenced by Google's ownership of YouTube and Google+, two of the world's best social networks. Google's algorithms are looking at social signals as one of the 200 factors that it assesses when ranking content on its search engine. Social Media Marketing includes all of the activities done to generate more fans, followers, and interaction.

Social Promotion is more about Google's perception of you and improved keyword placement.
Both social media marketing and social promotion are beneficial for ranking and traffic for your
website. Social Media is about relationship building. Make sure that you like and share content that your customers will appreciate. There has to be a balance with blatant sales pitches and
sharing entertaining and useful content. Simply put, people do business with people that they like.

Let's look at Social Media Marketing in depth now.

    (a) **Facebook**

Facebook is the world's largest social network that includes a huge swath of society on its platform. Facebook allows you to share web page links, images, text, and videos.

Facebook for business is another huge topic alone. Facebook is good for SEO because you can target your best prospective customer demographic through Facebook Groups, Facebook events, Facebook Ads, and business pages.

For maximum visibility on Facebook, it helps to cultivate relationships. You want your Facebook page information to be complete. If you own a Facebook Group, the same principle applies. Going beyond just a Facebook Business page means making sure that your Facebook business page has filled out all information. When you post status updates you should use no more than 2 hashtags for maximum visibility. You can follow me by liking www.facebook.com/theseoqueen.

Figure 19 Results of Organic Facebook Group Marketing

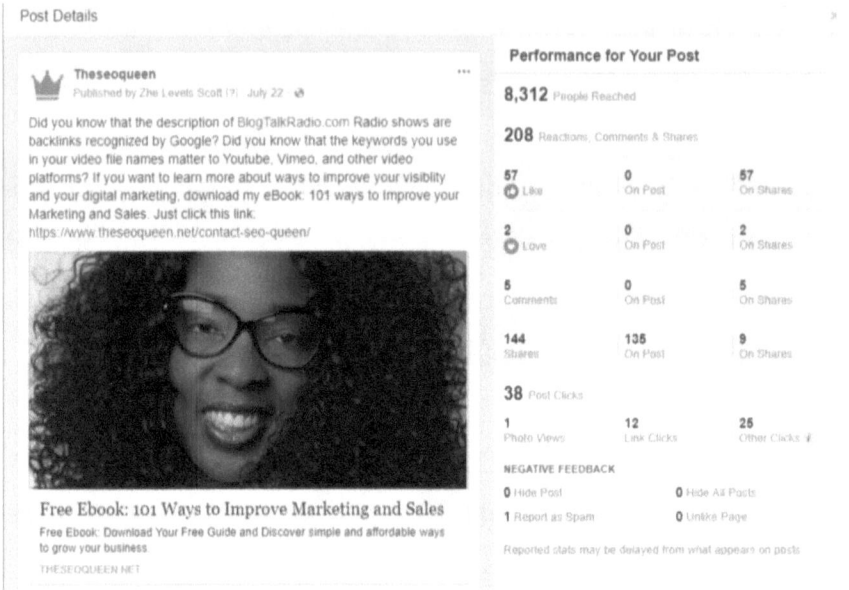

Takeaway: Think about what type of things that your ideal customer likes to do. Take me for an example. I know that business owners are my ideal prospects. I have a B to B business model. As a result, I will join Facebook groups that have business owners in it. Once you know what your ideal customers are, search on Facebook and join 5 groups. Read the rules of the group, and then start building relationships! Remember, people buy from those the know, like and trust!

(b) **Twitter**

Twitter is a very dynamic social network. You can really search for topics by hashtag. Twitter is great because google indexes your tweets and you really can interact with new people easily. There are not as many privacy restrictions as Facebook with interactions. Twitter limits all tweets to a maximum of 140 characters. So, it is important that you use Twitter to communicate with your customers and prospects succinctly. The optimal number of hashtags in a tweet is 1-2 hashtags. You can follow me @ZheTheSeoQueen.

 **Takeaway: Create a Twitter account. Make sure that your business page is linked to in your account description. Then start tweeting and interacting. Make sure that you share links to your website.**

(c) **Periscope**

Is a fairly new social network. This channel reminds me of Snap Chat, and Facebook's Live functionality. You have to have to a Twitter account to use Periscope. Each Periscope broadcast is available for unlimited viewing up to 24 hours after the initial broadcast. You can interact with your audience in real time as you are broadcasting. One great thing to do is to verbally acknowledge those who are watching.

This is a great way to build brand loyalty. Periscope is great because you can Name your broadcast and it shows up on a map. There is a website called https://katch.me/ that you can also link your periscope to that will record and store your periscope broadcast in the cloud for a long time.

(d) **YouTube**

YouTube is video search engine. Only 9% of small business owners are generating content to leverage this platform. This statistic is a golden opportunity for you to get on YouTube Video Results Page 1. This platform gets 700 million people visiting YouTube every month.

This is a goldmine of traffic for the savvy business owner. Creating video content and optimizing how you post it is very important for generating referral traffic to your website. You can generate referral traffic to your website by following the directions in the YouTube Optimization Template that I have created and included in this book. The Bonus about video marketing is that your digital assets will appear 52% more of the time on Google Page 1 when you use video marketing as a very important part of your digital marketing strategies.

YOUTUBE Optimization Template

In summary, whether you are loading a video on YouTube, Vimeo, Daily Motion, or some other video sharing platform make sure you include your link in the video description, make sure you include your link in the video, use your Keywords in the

Video File Name, Video Title, Tags, and Description. When users are looking for your company, you want to make sure that you are using the verbiage that they would use to find you.

 **Takeaway: Create a YouTube account. Upload a video using the YouTube Optimization Guidelines outlined. Follow TSQ Marketing Inc Channel on YouTube.**

(e) **Instagram**

Instagram is a photo and video sharing platform. You can use Instagram to share your company photos, memes, and infographics. An infographic is a picture that tells a story or teaches something. A great meme that I like is the Search Engine Land SEO Periodic Table. This is one of my favorite infographics because it takes a complex topic and summarizes it in less than 10,000 square pixels. Creating meaningful infographics for your business is a worthwhile endeavor because it shows how you are an expert in your vertical in a succinct way. 11 hashtags are the optimal number of hashtags for one post on Instagram. You can go to hashtagify.me to research your very best hashtags.

(f) **Pinterest**

Pinterest, like Instagram is a place where you can share images. However, Pinterest allows you to link the image to the URL of your choice. Because this platform is both a social network and a social bookmarking site, you get social signals and link juice when you pin your entire site to this website. In order for you to get backlinks and the social signals required for Google Page 1, you must utilize Pinterest. It is low hanging fruit for your digital marketing campaign. You can even use http://social.branding.graphicbrown.com/ to automate the posting of content to Pinterest and other social networks. Pinterest is ideal because it is a great source of referral traffic, and you can build a decent funnel to a squeeze/landing page of your choice.

(g) **LinkedIn**

This social network is very professional. You can share images, blog posts, LinkedIn exclusive content, videos and more. LinkedIn in has acronyms spelled: L.I.O.N. This means that a person who has identified themselves as a LION is a LinkedIn Open networker. This a great way to meet new people and expand your professional network. In addition, LinkedIn is a great source of referral traffic and full of prospects. Post updates with links to your target website. Share your website as appropriate in Groups. Share your website as a link on your LinkedIn Company and Personal profile(s).

Takeaway: Create a LinkedIn account. Share your video that you uploaded on YouTube on your LinkedIn Profile. Join 5 groups, and contribute value in the discussions. Connect with me on LinkedIn, and let me know what you think of this book here: https://www.linkedin.com/in/seoconsultantzhescott

(h)   **Google+**

Google's response to Facebook. Google+, although it is small, has valuable social signals that you do not want to miss out on. Share you content from your website and Facebook on Google+ this will help boost your rankings, and if you have followers that are searching for your content Google will serve your relevant Google + result to them.

(i)   **Tumblr**

This is an image/blogging platform that is very popular with young people.

(j)   **R**eddit

This is a discussion based platform where you can share text and links. This is a great platform to generate buzz.

Takeaway: Visit every social media website and get an idea for how it works and write 1 sentence about how each social network could help you. Also search on each platform using the Hashtags #ZheTheSeoQueen #LadyZhe so you can see how a hashtag works

ZHE L. Scott

SEO TRAINING 2017:
Search Engine Optimization & Marketing for Small Business

Available on Amazon

Traffic and Troubleshooting

1) Traffic and Troubleshooting: Many people look at websites as something that should never have problems. However, a website is like a building. Just like a building must stay up to code and requires repairs and updates, websites are precisely the same. As technology continues to advance and change it requires a flexible mind set.

2) The way your website is put together also determines how well your website will rank. The more SEO friendly the website platform the easier it is to make the necessary changes. As a business owner or marketing professional you can use the website cmsmatrix.org to compare the features of any Website Content Management System that you are considering. The content management system I would like to analyze is WordPress. You can look at the features on cmsmatrix.org by visiting: http://cmsmatrix.org/matrix/cms-matrix/wordpress. The thing that makes the WordPress website content management system highly effective is because you can optimize the site for content and maximum performance on the server. WordPress is able manage: Load Balancing, Page Caching, Advanced Caching, Database Replication, and Static Content Export. This is great when you have to change hosting companies as your company grows and your website needs become more sophisticated and expensive.

3) WordPress is also great because you can customize everything from your URL structure to your meta tags, headers, and more. This content management system is extremely flexible and SEO Friendly.

4) Now one content management system that I run across that many people turn too is WIX. WIX is a free website building platform available at wix.com. The problem I used to encounter with wix.com is that you cannot customize your URL structure and get rid of characters like #! Now the URL structure is very SEO friendly. However, it is very difficult to scan a WIX website with tools. Google is able to rank WIX sites, but WordPress sites rank easier due to their ease of analysis with automated tools. WIX may seem nice to start out with, but please note that you will not be able to have the flexibility as you do with WordPress.

Takeaway: Go to cmsmarix.org and compare the features of your current website management system to WordPress. Create a backup plan for the actual website files on your server and implement it for your website.

Tracking and Analytics Tools

Did you know that you can track the following statistics about your website visitors?

Country of origin	City of origin
Time spent on site	What pages they viewed
How keyword led them to your site	What keywords yield engaged visitors
What Google Search Engine Result page you are coming up for	What keywords your website ranks for
What browser is used most to access your site	What operating system is used most to access your site
What social media channel led them to your site	What ISP and cell phone provider brought them to your site.

You can even track demographics!

As a small business owner, this information is a gold mine for empirical evidence on your site's effectiveness. This information, when used correctly can help you optimize your website's effectiveness. In general, a great website has a conversion rate of 5%. This means that if your website is generating 100 hits per day, 5 of those visitors will become customers. As a result, this is a great benchmark to use when analyzing your data. In addition, the average website has a bounce rate of 50%. If your bounce rate is higher than 50%, then you know that you have a disconnect with you and your website audience.

You can use Google Analytics on your website and Google Webmaster tools to both track visitors and communicate with google about indexing your website.

One Last Thing…

Have you found **value** and **benefit** from reading this book?

Do you think others struggling with their marketing strategy would find a **benefit** from reading this book?

Would you be prepared to **recommend** my book to others, or be prepared to write a positive review about it?

Who would be the first two people that you know who are self-employed or running their own business, that might benefit from reading this kindle book too?

I really hope you have got value from my book. You definitely will if you choose to take action, and start using some of the tools, resources and information I've shared.

Take a moment, reflect on this book and write down the top 5 key "takeaways" you've gained from this book. Write what you've learned and consider adding a review of the book, for amazing things are about to start happening when you begin

embracing and applying the principles contained herein, and my other books.

In addition to adding a review, consider sharing your thoughts via your online networks such as LinkedIn, Facebook and twitter. If you believe the book is worth sharing, please would you take a few seconds to let your friends know about it? If it turns out to make a difference in their lives and businesses, they'll be forever grateful to you, as will I.

You can add your review by revisiting our product page in the Amazon Kindle Store.

Click on "Create Your Own Review" then claim your **FREE** membership in the SEO Queen Mastermind Group by visiting: www.facebook.com/groups/TheSeoQueen to meet and connect with other like-minded individuals all sharing and applying the knowledge and strategies that I share in this book.

About the Author

Zhe L. Scott is a HubSpot Certified Inbound Marketer and Digital Marketing Certification Associate Faculty Member for Simplilearn, one of the world's largest online learning communities. She is also a founding member of Grow Your Business Club and Veteran Digital Marketing Warrior. She built her first website in 1996 as an undergraduate at the Massachusetts Institute of Technology. During her time at MIT she was awarded the Burchard Scholar award and the Albert G Hill Prize for improving minority student life at MIT. After Graduation Zhe L. Scott worked for Fortune 500 company Raytheon developing web based applications and also the Federal Bureau of Investigations as an honors intern during the Summer of 2003.

This is her first book on Digital marketing, and second overall. You can download her free eBook: 101 Ways to Improve Your Marketing and Sales by visiting www.theseoqueen.net/contact-seo-queen. This book is a culmination of the many years of consulting, optimizing and fighting for high keyword placement for 100s of companies worldwide. From companies in China, Australia, Asia, Europe, and the United States of America. Zhe L. Scott has seen and accomplished tons of keyword rankings and traffic for her clients. You can view a sample of her Google Page Rankings by visiting this link: https://youtu.be/eiS3WMJDh8I. She has managed 200+ Digital marketing campaigns successfully where her clients appeared and stayed on Google Page 1.

Zhe L. Scott has advised 1,000s of companies on the best course of action with their digital marketing campaigns and has been blogging about search engine optimization since 2010.

Zhe Scott is the President and founder of TSQ Marketing Inc which was established in January 2017. Zhe Scott has also spoken at conferences on the topic of digital marketing and more.

The mission of TSQ Marketing Inc is to empower businesses to reach their full revenue potential through demand generation and demand optimization. THE SEO QUEEN helps companies get their share of the 1.2 Trillion Searches that are happening on Google alone, and get to the top of their niche. Please connect with Zhe L. Scott on social media for more great content:

https://www.facebook.com/theSeoQueen/
https://twitter.com/ZheTheSeoQueen/
https://www.linkedin.com/in/seoconsultantzhescott/
https://www.pinterest.com/tsqmarketinginc/
http://instagram.com/ZheTheSeoQueen/

If you have questions or comments please email me directly at info@theseoqueen.net or visit the site at theseoqueen.net or of course you can also connect with me directly by visiting my LinkedIn profile at https://www.linkedin.com/in/seoconsultantzhescott

Other Work by the Author

For more, visit: www.theseoqueen.net/contact-seo-queen

Credits

Photography by Regina Kimball, Graphic Design by www.facebook.com/SeeYourReign, Styling and Makeup by Zhe L. Scott

YouTube Channel Music by Lady Zhe
ladyzhe.bandcamp.com | www.ladyzhe.com | www.facebook.com/ladyzhe

Need More Website Traffic?

https://www.theseoqueen.net/reach-more-clients-power-session/

The following services are available from TSQ Marketing Inc:

- **Technical SEO** – This is ideal for websites on WordPress, Shopify, Magento or another highly technical website content management system. ($750 or $1500 per month with or without link building)
- **CMO In a Box** – Chief Marketing Officer in A Box is everything and the kitchen sink. SEO, Conversion Optimization, Social Media Marketing, Email Marketing, Marketing Automation and Website management are all included ($15,000 per month). You can sign up for this program by booking a Reach More Clients Power Session to verify that this package is the best fit for your business goals: https://www.theseoqueen.net/reach-more-clients-power-session/

- **Digital Marketing Academy** – Want to Study Directly with Zhe Scott and build lucrative digital marketing skills? This program is the one for you. It is only $997/month and you can sign up by visiting: https://theseoqueen.net/digital-marketing-academy/

https://www.theseoqueen.net/reach-more-clients-power-session/

www.ingramcontent.com/pod-product-compliance
Lightning Source LLC
Chambersburg PA
CBHW030906180526
45163CB00004B/1734